HOW TO WRITE
AWESOME DIALOGUE!
for fiction, film and theatre

Techniques from
a published author and theatre guy

HOW TO WRITE AWESOME DIALOGUE!
for fiction, film and theatre

Techniques from
a published author and theatre guy

Tom Leveen

FTJ Creative LLC
Scottsdale, Arizona

www.tomleveen.com

First edition: May 2015

ISBN-13: 978-1511742634
ISBN-10: 1511742631

Printed in U.S.A

What people are saying about Tom Leveen's dialogue, voice, and character:

Party (Random House, 2010)

"I must say that I'm absolutely **in awe of Leveen's ability to build such distinct and totally believable voice** for eleven characters in one novel."
~ fortheloveofya.com

Zero (Random House, 2012)

"Well written, **with a distinct and fantastically done voice**, Zero is an unflinching must read."
~ agoodaddiction.blogspot.com

"[H]is **voice is fresh and strong and consistent**."
~ scratchingcat.wordpress.com

"Part of **what makes the book, and the voice, believable** is Leveen's ability to channel a teenage girl and make her real. It's all there—the insecurity, the bravado, the conflicting feelings about sex, the sense that your whole life is in front of you, which is both exhilarating and paralyzing."
~ The *Phoenix New Times*

manicpixiedreamgirl (Random House, 2013)

"[I]t's the **relationships between the novel's teenage characters that are the real standouts**. Tyler's crass banter with his buddies, his snarky but supportive relationship with his sister, and his botched dealings with both Becky and Sydney are **entirely realistic**."
~ Publisher's Weekly

"Tom Leveen has **a unique voice** and writes interesting male characters, so I was intrigued to check out his latest book *manicpixiedreamgirl*. Leveen's characters are usually creative types and not the typical leading men you see in YA....I thought the male voice in *manicpixiedreamgirl* was very strong and unique."
~ thereadingdate.com

Random (Simon Pulse, 2014)

"Author Tom Leveen presents a powerful story with **a plot so real**, readers will be gripped from the very first page."
~ readingjunky.blogspot.com

Sick (Abrams/Amulet, 2013)

"[Leveen] **really nails the 'guy' dialogue** as well—it is gross, colorful, and at times, downright funny."
~ VOYA (Voice of Youth Advocates)

"In an exciting take on the zombie novel, Leveen … shifts to horror while maintaining **his trademark complex relationships and character-driven storytelling**."
~ Publisher's Weekly

"Tom Leveen's voice is truly one of the best elements…"
~ blog.homoeoteleuton.com

Table of Contents

Part Three – On the Page

Part Four – Narration

Part Five - Conclusions

Introduction

I *love* teaching this class! That's what this book is: A class including some of the tips and techniques of writing dialogue that similar guides might not address. Nothing against those books—you should read those, too! I certainly do.

But *this* writing book . . . I think this one is different because few authors bring more than two decades of theatre experience to the word processor. That experience permanently influenced how I perceive, read, and write dialogue.

I've taught the contents of this book at comic book conventions, junior and senior high schools, professional writers' conferences, universities, private writing groups, bookstores—you name it. In a sense, I spent about five years creating this book; refining some material, cutting some out, adding new stuff as I learn it. (That's lesson number one— you never stop learning!)

I believe my theatre background helped enormously in the sale of my first novel, *Party*, to an imprint of Random House. More importantly, I believe it can help you strengthen your dialogue, too—an aspect oft-bemoaned by editors and agents as lacking in fiction manuscripts.

Real quick: As with any book or class on writing, this is not gospel. Take what you like, leave the rest. These are not rules, and if they were, you can find hundreds of novels that break them. That's fine; I break them, too! The point is to find useful bits that will help your writing, and in turn, help you sell it, whether that's directly to an e-reader site or to a legacy publisher like Random House, Simon & Schuster, and so on.

In other words, there are exceptions to absolutely everything I'm about to show you. Overall, though, I believe the vast majority of these techniques, ideas, and ways of looking at your novel will be helpful as you write and revise.

Very little of this information, by the way, is original to me. This book represents a synthesis of more than twenty years of experience I've gained from other directors and actors, coaches, teachers, screenwriters, editors, agents...you name it. I owe them each a great deal of thanks.

One final note:

It's my belief that the information contained in this book is *primarily for revision*. After your fifth or sixth novel, it might come more naturally during the writing of a fresh new story, but until it does, don't worry about any of this information while you write a first draft. It'll just get confusing. Get that first draft done, then print it out and set it beside this book with pencil in hand to take notes on your manuscript.

Ready? Let's speak the speech!

~ Tom Leveen
May, 2015

A Note On Scripts

I am often asked by students, "Do you want your books to become movies?" The answer is, absolutely! Adults often ask, "Have you adapted your books to screenplays or for the stage because of your background in theatre?" The answer is, absolutely not!

This book can help writers of novels, short stories, screenplays, teleplays, or stage plays, because the information is fundamental to plots, conflict, character development, and the things characters say.

Writing scripts for film, television, or theatre each require different skill sets and are different arts than prose fiction, though. Even the short story is a much different animal than the novel.

I'll stand by the information you're about to read as being useful for any format of storytelling. If you are writing your first script, however, I encourage you to read widely on the topic in addition to using this text.

PART ONE – PLOT

Awesome Dialogue Starts with Plot & Conflict

Writing awesome dialogue begins with an awesome plot.

Awesome here needn't mean *original*. For our purposes, it merely means strong. Well-defined. Clear.

Awesome dialogue springs from

awesome plots because

awesome plots have

awesome conflict.

(*Awesome!*)

For now, we'll define plot simply as "What happens in the story." Cool?

Cool. So then, what is conflict?

Two forces wanting exactly opposite things.

Jaws and Chief Brody. Luke and Darth Vader. Romeo and Capulet. Outer space and the crew of *Apollo 13*.

Notice I don't use the word "people" in this definition. You've heard of man vs. man, man vs. himself, and man vs. nature? A "force" can be any of those things; anything that is an obstacle to the character getting what she wants.

Prove it! a.k.a. Actionable Goals

A strong plot—and thus, strong dialogue—begins with the character having an *actionable goal*. This is sometimes called the Want or the Need.

An actionable goal ought to be tangible. That is to say:

An actionable goal is something the reader can prove was or was not obtained or accomplished by the character.

The point of the actionable goal is for the author to specify what exactly will constitute success or failure on the part of the character. Some goals are implicit to the story, some are stated directly. But every character in your novel has one. They are often simple statements, such as "I want to go to prom with Billy," or "I want to slay the dragon of Eversplat."

My first novel, *Party*, has eleven chapters, and each chapter is told from a different character's point of view. As a result, I needed to come up with an actionable goal for each narrator, because each is, in a sense, one of eleven protagonists.

Take a look at this portion of chapter one:

> **This becomes my new motivation: Go to the party. Walk around. See if anyone, just one person, says my name. Says "Hi!" Says "I had Spanish with you sophomore year."** (*Party*, p.12)

There it is. An actionable goal. The narrator, a girl named Beckett, has just decided what she wants, and how she plans to get it. Her actionable goal might not seem as colossal as, say, "slay the dragon," except that in the context of *her story*, slaying a dragon is exactly what she's doing, *metaphorically*. Her goal is still proveable: To see if anyone says hello.

The second chapter is narrated by a sassy, punk-minded teen named Morrigan, who has a less-than-stellar relationship with her parents. I knew her Want—her *actionable goal*—needed to be related to that central issue.

The first goal I came up with was: "Morrigan wants her dad to love her."

Nice. Nothing wrong with it. The problem is, I cannot *prove* it to you. I cannot show you by the end of the novel whether or not Morrigan obtains this Want. It's too nebulous. I can imply, infer, and illustrate . . . but the reader cannot prove it conclusively.

Okay. Second attempt: "Morrigan wants her dad to notice her."

Better, but still not concrete. Still a little vague in terms of what I can show you on the written page. Her dad can "see" her without truly noticing her, so showing him having a conversation with her doesn't prove he has noticed her in the way she needs him to.

So my final decision was: "Morrigan wants her dad to hug her."

That is something I can prove happened or did not happen. It also suggests elements of the first two Wants: to be loved and to be noticed. Of course, a hug doesn't prove Dad loves her, but that isn't the point. What's important is that she has a goal and takes action to obtain it.

It's okay if the Want is implied. We can get a sense of what characters are after simply by the actions they take. Morrigan does not state outright, "I want my dad to hug me!" But by the time it either happens or does not happen, readers will know what it is she wanted. What's important is that you, creator-god of the story, have that actionable goal in mind.

Wishful Thinking

Notice we don't allow the character to indulge in "wishful thinking." There is a difference between a wish and a Want or a Need. "I wish my dad would hug me" doesn't have the import, the gravitas, that a Want, Need, or Goal has.

In fiction, wishes are rather "wishy-washy."

Could you write an entire story about a character who says this: "I wish I didn't have to go to work today so I could go to the beach." More importantly, would you *read* one? Would anybody?

Probably not. Why? Because, well, just don't go to work. Just don't! There might be consequences for failing to show up at his job, but no one's got a gun to his head. Have him toddle on off to the beach if you like. In short: quit whining!

But what if he says instead, "I want to go to the beach today."

That's a declaration of intent, that's something he can fight for, and something we can know either happens or does not happen. It is either achieved or not achieved. This is an actionable goal.

Ah, but what if he says this: "I'm going to the beach today, and nothing is going to stop me!"

Now *that's* a plot (once you add in some obstacles). A story about going to the beach may or may not be full of dire intrigue, but it's a whole lot better than merely whining, *I wish I didn't hafta go to work today.*

See the difference?

Let's say we have a high school boy, Timmy, the protagonist of a young adult contemporary novel, who narrates: "I wish Brittany liked me."

That's nice. Good for you, Timmy. But it's *passive*. It's not a Want. I can't prove conclusively yes she does or no she doesn't like him back. Again, I can infer, or imply, or illustrate, but cannot *prove*.

Maybe she publicly insults him to hide that she likes him. Maybe she sends him love letters only to make her ex-boyfriend jealous. Being insulted and getting love letters do not prove whether she likes him or not.

Yet merely replacing "wish" with "want" doesn't help here. Saying "I *want* Brittany to like me" faces the same problem: it can't be proven that she does or does not.

So the author asks, *What would prove that she likes you?* To which Timmy says, "Well, she'd, I dunno, gimme a kiss."

Then what he Wants is *for her to kiss him*. That is actionable. "Kiss" is the strong verb we're looking for. We will know, in no uncertain terms, whether or not Brittany has kissed Timmy by the time the story ends.

Protagonists Should Take Charge

But wait—there's something mildly awry with both the Kissing Brittany example and the Hugging Dad example.

These actionable goals rely on *another* character to take action. To have a strong plot, these should be rephrased as:

I want to hug my dad.

and

I want to kiss Brittany.

Or, to offer a third example:

I want to destroy the One Ring. As opposed to, "I want the One Ring destroyed."

Rephrased this way, the results of pursuing those Goals are squarely in the hands of the protagonist, where they belong.

Strong plots come from protagonists who take action. Stated or implied, they have a Want, and they go after it

with absolutely everything they've got. It's a matter of life or death.

Sometimes that's literal, as in *The Hunger Games*. Sometimes it's social or metaphorical, as in a bubble gum young adult romance. (I shall not name any here…)

The protagonist must Want something and pursue it. Your job is to make that as hard on them as possible. That's what makes a strong plot.

Making things difficult for the protagonist is, of course, simply another way of saying…

Create conflict.

Conflict

Every character—main, secondary, walk-on; protagonist, antagonist, villain—*wants something.*

Without a Want, there can be no conflict.

Without conflict, there is no story.

Without story, clever dialogue only sits on the page looking pretty, but accomplishing nothing. (Ask me how I know.)

Pretend you know absolutely nothing about the story of Romeo and Juliet and are reading it for the first time in the form of a novel. Call it *Montague's War.*

Right off the bat: A brilliant opening scene in which factions of the Montague and Capulet clans get into a street fight. Each force wants opposite things: to kill the other!

Blam! *Conflict.*

Now a few pages later, still in the first scene (the first "chapter," let's say) Romeo makes his appearance. What do we know by the end of the scene? He's a hopeless romantic, and we can feel or predict that he's going to get into some kind of trouble with a woman. Maybe it'll be Rosaline, who—we discover only later—never even shows up in the story. It's not until we meet Juliet that we experience the *ah-ha*! moment that correlates to our prediction. Romeo and Juliet are going to hook up. (Ignore for the moment the original title of the story, of course.) We know there will be sparks between them, we can see it coming a mile away.

After we've met Romeo, are we even a tiny bit surprised that he falls hard for this other girl at a dance? Not at all.

Now hearken back to that first scene:

The author ties the opening fight to the main plot. It's not just a street brawl for the sake of an action sequence. It's a fight illustrating for us how deep the rift runs between these two families. The mere fact that Shakespeare includes it tells us immediately the feud is going to play a big role in things to come. Once we meet Juliet Capulet, the boulder has been pushed off the cliff: we know there's no turning back and there's going to be trouble. Big trouble. Just how big, we don't know, but we hope these two kids will make it through alive, if not together.

If we didn't know the story already, we might in fact *expect* them to live happily ever after, since it's a "romance."

Before we reach Scene/Chapter 2, we already have a sense of conflict, and of Romeo's Want. His tangible Want (his actionable goal) is to be with Rosaline; his implied Want (as discussed by his buddies) *to be in love*. His actionable goal changes when he meets Juliet. Later, we see him and Juliet take specific actions to obtain their Want (to be together, or to get married), while all around them, people are throwing up barriers to stop them. Certainly Tybalt is one such obstacle; Juliet's father another. Romeo's buddies first endeavor to make him forget about Rosaline (and, by teasing him into attending Capulet's party, thus accidentally trigger the plot point that will propel the rest of the story). Nothing is wasted or accidental or incidental.

Point being, Romeo and Juliet's relationship is surrounded by conflict . . . just as it should be to make a compelling plot.

Conflicts must be created to thwart your characters' goals. If you've got clearly established conflicts, your dialogue will automatically bump itself up a notch, because the characters will by default be talking about the conflict around them, and so the plot moves forward.

Lovers and Fighters

In *Audition* (Bantam, 1978), his classic text for actors on auditioning for film and theatre, Michael Shurtleff writes, "A story full of people fighting for something is much better" than a story with people who want to leave or avoid a difficult situation or scene.

Scrutinizing your characters for their Wants, Needs, or Goals is always a good move. Even better, though, is to make the characters *fight for* them.

While it may seem a matter of semantics, using the verb "fight" can clarify for you, the author, just how badly your characters are trying to achieve their goals. *Fight* has an intensity and focus that "want" or "need" does not. These semantics are important for you as the author because it helps underscore just how important the goal must be.

For instance, compare:

I want to hug my dad.
I want to kiss Brittany.

Versus:

I'm going to fight to hug my dad.
I'm going to fight to kiss Brittany.

Taste the difference?

While your protagonist may never (and probably should never) say out loud, "I'm going to fight to kiss Brittany!" phrasing it in this manner in your own notes should help you keep that Actionable Goal front and center.

It should also remind you, as creator-god of the story, *to fight back against the protagonist.* Remember, it's your job to make his life as difficult as possible under the given circumstances of the story.

One final note on this: Take care not to "play the end of the play." Particularly in revision, *you* may know the ending of the story, but the characters don't. The characters should be fighting for what they want every step of the way, without knowing whether they'll get it or not. (*Romeo & Juliet* is again a great example: Imagine the actors playing the roles like they know they're going to die at the end?)

What's On The Agenda?

Characters do not speak unless they want something.

Each speaking character has an agenda. Every line they say out loud advances that agenda.

That's not to say that every line should be, "Hug me! Hug me!" or "I'm destroying the ring! I'm destroying the ring!"

It just means that if you are going to give a character space to speak up, it's got to be because she wants something.

Prince Swordbender's actionable goal may well be to kill the Abominable Sandman of Philadelphia; but when he complains to his team of misfit adventurers who've joined his quest that his feet are aching as they march, he Wants something else in that moment—perhaps to:

Hear some sympathy so he knows he's not as alone as he feels;

Lay the groundwork of maybe getting a foot massage from the nymph Gigglebottom (and maybe something more later tonight, *wacka-chicka, wacka-chicka*);

Merely hear the sound of his own voice since leaving the Forest of Silence.

Point being, the prince has an agenda as soon as he says, "My feet hurt." Any of these examples—even if they seem silly at first—can and should be tied to his overall actionable goal, or at least a subplot of it.

If, on the other hand, there is no real connection to the story—developing character, theme, or the plot—then maybe Swordbender's foot pain should stay in the narrative rather than in dialogue.

We are constantly choosing what to say and what not to say in real life (some of us more and better than others). So too should your characters. Your novel can't afford characters who talk just to hear themselves talk.

The talk has to matter.

Think of advancing the agenda as a series of rungs on a ladder leading to the big showdown of the novel. Each rung is critical right then and there, because without it, the character (and story) might fall. But the goal is always up there, in sight, and your protagonist is fighting to get to it.

You Are The Star

Sir Anthony Hopkins, famous movie star extraordinaire, told an anecdote about being in a play with Sir Laurence Olivier when Hopkins was a young actor. Hopkins went to Olivier one evening before the show for advice on a monologue:

"[Olivier] said, 'You're the star of the show.' I said, 'What?' He said, 'Well, you're the only one speaking at the moment.'"

When a character speaks, he or she is the star of the show.

As a stage veteran of more than twenty years, I can tell you this advice is true. No matter how many people are on stage, *whoever is speaking is the person the audience is looking at.* For that one moment, even a walk-on spear-carrier who shouts, "M'lord!" is a star.

The same is true in your novel when it comes to dialogue. Readers do not, for example, simply skip over lines of dialogue spoken by the server in the restaurant who asks the protagonist if she'd like more coffee. Readers assume, rightly, that if a character speaks, the line must be important. Make sure it is!

What the Hopkins anecdote emphasizes for us as writers is this: If a character speaks, he is the star of that moment, no matter how brief, and no matter how little he says.

What's that mean for us? Ask yourself if the server *should* be given a line. Her one line of dialogue—"Can I get you some more coffee?"—has to serve a purpose, or it shouldn't be there.

When she speaks, she is the star. Do you want her upstaging or interrupting the scene happening between your two main characters?

(The answer might be "Yes!")

I'm not suggesting you cut out any character who only has a line or two of dialogue. On the contrary, I'm pointing out that if a character—walk-on or otherwise—is going to take

up valuable real estate (i.e. space on the page) in your novel, then his words need to serve a purpose.

For example:

Imagine an ex-husband and ex-wife in a breakfast restaurant. The server approaches in the middle of their scene and says, "Can I get you some more coffee?"

Does her interruption come at a key moment so your protagonist can use the distraction to sort out his thoughts? Or, perhaps, to pull a concealed weapon? (Hey, I don't know what kind of novel you're writing!)

Is the line delivered in such a way that the protagonist knows she's overheard their discussion and thinks he's a pig, which in turn makes him change how he's approaching the conversation?

Like every other choice we're talking about in this book, these one-line "stars" must be deliberate choices on your part.

Remember: The server has an agenda (getting a good tip, hurrying them along because it's the end of her shift, whatever). Your purpose in including her line of dialogue, however, is about pushing the story forward. She's the star when she speaks, but once she's done, the next character takes center stage again.

Genre Quirks

Speculative genre novels typically have a built-in Want, usually around a main villain. "I want to destroy the One Ring" or "I need to kill Kurgan by chopping off his head" for example.

In contemporary (non-supernatural, non-speculative) fiction, there's more room for subtlety in the phrasing of the Goal. Again, Morrigan's Want in *Party*—"I want my dad to hug me"—isn't stated outright, but it's in there (on page 28, in fact). Furthermore, with that Want in mind, you can see how she takes actions to get it. Most of them are harmful actions, or stupid actions, but they are *deliberate* actions.

A character's goals should usually be found in the first chapter in which the speaking character appears. It might be the main goal, or might not; if not, it should generally be related to the main goal. Romeo's main goal, for instance, doesn't come up until after he meets Juliet. When we first meet him, his goal is to be with Rosaline—again, this mirrors nicely with what will become his goal for the rest of the story.

In fairness, first chapters sometimes serve mostly to hook the reader with voice, character, action, or lovely description. That's fine. Do consider getting that actionable goal into the text as quickly as possible, though.

Part One Q & A

Q: Must the protagonist obtain his Want by the end of the story?

A: No. Romeo and Juliet don't. Hamlet does, but (spoiler alert!) still gets himself killed, which should easily fall into the "no" column. Whether your protagonist obtains the Want doesn't matter nearly as much as how hard she strives to obtain it. The harder she works for it, the more difficult it is, the more exciting your story will be.

"Exciting" does not have to mean "swashbuckling." You could write (and I have read) more than one story about something as simple as, say, a fan trying to meet a movie star that had nothing by way of combat, explosions, or other "action," yet was a novel that could not be put down.

I couldn't put it down because the protagonist's goal was clear, and she pursued it relentlessly, no matter what got in her way . . . and something got in her way every other page or so.

Q: You mean I can't just have walk-ons who do and say what walk-ons normally would? Doesn't this add flavor or texture to the scenes?

A: Sure, you can, and it does. But be aware how such additions impact non-dialogue aspects of the story, such as pacing. For example, let's go back to our divorced couple in the restaurant:

> **"He's my son, too!"** Frank said. **"Either you give me partial custody, or—"**

"Can I get you some more coffee?" the waitress interrupted, appearing by the table with a smile and a fresh pot of joe.

Frank glared up at her and barked, "No!" This made the waitress, a girl of maybe nineteen, look pouty and stomp away.

"And you wonder why I don't want to give you partial custody," Judy said.

"I'm taking you to court," Frank said.

The server's appearance and dialogue directly impact the scene. Better still, Frank is now at a disadvantage, and will have to fight (there's that word, *fight*) harder to make his case.

Now compare it to this version:

"He's my son, too!" Frank said. "Either you give me partial custody, or—"

"Can I get you some more coffee?" the waitress interrupted, appearing by the table with a smile and a fresh pot of joe.

Frank and Judy shook their heads.

"Or I'll take you to court," Frank went on.

In this example, the server's appearance doesn't mean anything. She adds nothing to the scene, apart from establishing the setting is in a diner . . . which should have been handled at the beginning of the scene anyway, not in the middle.

In the Civil War film *Glory*, the 54th Massachusetts Volunteer Infantry—the North's first all-black regiment—has been beset by constant racism by the ranks of their own Union soldier brothers-in-arms. That is, right up until the moment before the final battle of the film when a white Union solider shouts, "Give 'em hell, Fifty-four!"

It's a goosebump-raising moment. This guy has one line; four words; six syllables. Yet it tells us (and the regiment, for that matter) how things have changed since the story started. That one, nameless character impacts the entire story *because* he is one, nameless character. It might have worked just fine if one of the other principal characters said it . . . but it would have lacked the punch delivered here.

His words, in the context of the story, matter deeply.

Q: You said Romeo's actionable goal changes from Rosaline to Juliet. Is it okay to do that? Just change the Want mid-stream?

A: It's okay to change the Want, yes; to do it mid-stream, no. Romeo's shift happens before the end of Act One, for example. The bulk of the story is about marrying Juliet, not Rosaline. His goal to "obtain" Rosaline is important because it introduces us to Romeo as a character: We know that when he falls in love, he falls hard and he falls fast. The initial Want is directly tied into character, but quickly switches to the Want he'll be pursuing for the rest of the story.

Consider *Raiders of the Lost Ark* as a contemporary example of the same. We see Indiana Jones pursing a Want (the Hovitos idol) that illustrates many aspects of his character, but that Goal only takes up about 10 minutes of screen time. His actionable goal is about obtaining the ark and takes up most of the story time. And, like *Romeo & Juliet*, this opening goal also introduces the story's main antagonists—Tybalt in the former, Belloq in the latter.

These short opening sequences show concrete, actionable goals for the protagonists while also laying a lot of plot and character groundwork. Oh, that we could all be so efficient!

Exercises

I'm not a huge fan of writing exercises myself, so I won't be hurt if you skip these. But some people really do enjoy them and make crucial discoveries by using them—for you, I include these.

1. Print out a scene from your story. Use a pen or pencil to mark where your protagonist is actively pursuing her goal by virtue of what she says.

Can't find any such moments? Guess what you get to do tonight! As Morgan Freeman says in *The Shawshank Redemption*, "Get busy revisin', or get busy dyin'."

. . . Well, words to that effect.

2. Very simply: Write down A) what your hero wants, B) what stands in his way, and C) what actions he takes to get it. (It's simple, but not always easy!) These three sentences can form not only the basis of a query letter and/or one-paragraph synopsis, but can also help you clarify your protagonist's actionable goals.

3. Find a scene with a walk-on character, whether he has spoken lines or not. Reverse the choice you currently have; if he speaks, delete his line (or character) and see what changes. If he doesn't have a line, give him one or two that will impact the scene in some way—a critical interruption, a piece of needed information, expressing an opinion on the scene . . . whatever. Whether you keep this walk-on character or not, did his involvement reveal anything new about the scene or characters you did not know before?

4. This one I've actually done and it did help:

Take two central characters from two of your different stories. (Not necessarily protagonists; just important characters. If you haven't written two stories, which I find hard to believe, choose one from a favorite book, movie, play, or TV show.)

Put these two characters in room together from which they cannot leave. (I used a windowless, doorless concrete bunker.) Maybe they're trying to figure out where they are, how they got here, or how to get out.

Let them talk. That's all. See where the conversation goes, see what relationships develop. Whose point of view did you choose? Did one or both characters reveal something here away from their "home pages" that you might not otherwise have known?

I used this exercise with a female space pirate character set 200 years in the future, and Amanda Walsh, my seventeen-year-old protagonist of *Zero*. I actually did learn some things about both women that I ended up using in their stories. Not the dialogue itself, just the revelations of character.

Which just goes to show—these are exercises. Again, take what you like, leave the rest.

PART TWO – SETTING THE STAGE

Things That Impact and Change Dialogue

Setting

Setting is the physical surroundings the characters are in. And setting always changes dialogue.

This may already come naturally to you, because it's a natural thing in our day-to-day life. Having a difficult conversation with a loved one comes out of our mouths one way if it's at the end of a long day at work than it does in the middle of a comfy Sunday picnic away from the kids.

While it may come naturally to us in real life, we must still take care to use setting deliberately in our stories. As with everything else we will discuss in this book, choosing your setting and how it impacts your dialogue is an intentional act on your part.

Where your scene is taking place impacts your dialogue as much as *what* is happening. Take a look at these two lines:

> **"Did you miss me?"**
> **"Shut up."**

Who did you immediately imagine? Men, women, boys, girls? (Dragons? Vampires? Sentient octopi?) All you have is two lines of dialogue—it could be anyone, anywhere.

Let's play with the setting. (We're playing with the characters, too, but don't mind that for now.)

1) Airport. Boyfriend and girlfriend who haven't seen each other all summer long. What happens next?

2) Airport. Ex-wife and ex-husband. He's there to pick up their son. They share joint custody of him. How does it sound?

3) High school. First day back after summer. Two football teammates meet at their lockers. What do you hear?

4) High school. First day back after summer. A bully and her victim pass in the hall. What's next?

No matter what images came to mind—none are right or wrong—I'm willing to bet most of us came up with similar tones of voice for each scenario. For example, did you envision a kiss coming up soon in example #1? Did you hear anger, derision, or dismissal in example #2? Were there some smiles in example #3, and perhaps mumbling—or defiance—in #4?

Now take a monologue like "Once more unto the breach" in *King Henry V*. This is typically set, rightly so, with Henry on a horse or perhaps a boulder or some other high place, urging his men on to victory, to not give up the fight. It's powerful and inspiring, usually given in a nice Kenneth Branagh accent (apropos, as he did a film version in 1989).

Here, I render it in a plain, unadorned prose:

Once more unto the breach, dear friends, once more; or close the wall up with our English dead. In peace, there's nothing so becomes a man as modest

stillness and humility. **But when the blast of war blows in our ears, then imitate the action of the tiger.**

In a novel, given that it's a big, rousing speech, perhaps with the sun high over head and Henry's army chomping at the bit to continue the fight, I might write it like this:

"Once more unto the breach, dear friends! Once more! Or close the wall up with our English dead!"

But.

What happens if, as creator-god of the story, you let Henry get his butt kicked the first time out, and the English must lay siege. And then, without changing a single word of the monologue, we put him hunkered around a tiny campfire; it's cold, and dark, with a quarter moon glaring down at them. And Henry, instead of shouting and cheering his entire army on into battle, instead gives the monologue to just a handful of his faithful but dispirited captains:

"Once more unto the breach, dear friends. *Once. More.* Or . . . close the wall up with our English dead."

Neither is better or worse, and I'm not suggesting you change things for change's sake. But do examine your settings; are you getting the most mileage out of your dialogue based on where the scene is set? When you choose a setting, how does it change how the dialogue is spoken?

(If you're wondering about the punctuation and font styles I chose for those examples, worry not—we'll get to that in a little bit.)

Consider another example:

You've got a 17-year-old boyfriend and girlfriend having the standard "define the relationship" discussion. (You know, "The Talk.")

Put them in his bedroom.

At night.

And no one else is home.

Hmm. Can you hear how that conversation might sound?

Now take the same characters and goals, and put them on a lonely suspension bridge out in the country, dangling their legs off the edge.

How about in the back of a speeding New York taxi during a thunderstorm?

Or on a playground on a sunny Sunday afternoon while they baby-sit his little brother?

Even if you did not change the words of the dialogue (or punctuation, or font), each location fundamentally changes how the scene is read and understood.

When you were a kid and wanted to ask for something big from your parents—your first car, or to go to a particular concert, maybe—you knew when and where to do the asking. Why? Because moods change with time and place. Show the same forethought with the scenes in your novel.

The Body and Dialogue

How your character is physically feeling impacts her dialogue.

On one fine Phoenix night, some friends and I were trespassing at a local middle school. We often did this. Because we were teenagers.

Anyway. We'd discovered that the ropes and chains on the flagpole were unsecured. We could grab the ropes, and swing high and around the pole like teenage tether balls. Trust me, we thought it was awesome. (At least we weren't ingesting anything illicit.)

Suddenly a police helicopter roared toward us, spotlight on and swinging our direction. We scurried for cover under the roof of the school's main walkway. Quickly, we decided two of the guys should run for the single pickup truck we'd taken to the school, while the rest of us raced to the back of the campus to get picked up.

All of us were either A) smokers or B) asthmatic at the time, so there was only so much running we could do before we were panting like dogs.

The searchlight scrambled across the ground as we raced full speed down an alley. One of my friends spotted a large black trash can. We decided to try and ditch the searchlight by hiding behind the trash can.

Pop quiz: Did he say the following?

"I believe we might wish to consider taking refuge, my friends. Perhaps we ought to conceal ourselves behind this garbage can, and lift the lid to provide additional cover from the searchlight."

Um, no. In actuality, he said this:

"Behind the garbage can! Behind it! Behind it, lift the lid up!"

His word choice, rhythm, and so on indicate his mental and physical state: out of breath, in a hurry, and maybe panicked.

(I have this entire episode on videotape, by the way, which is why I can tell you exactly what was said.)

There's a reason every action movie consists of lines like, *"Go! Run! Get down! Move! Get to the choppa!"* It's because there's a physiological response happening in our bodies when we are in a fight-or-flight situation. Our resources aren't devoted to thinking how to speak.

(By the way, that's the official spelling of "choppa," according to schwarzenegger.com.)

It's why when two guys are squaring off and puffing out their chests at a bar or ball game, getting ready to fight, their language not only gets uglier, but also shorter and clipped.

Their bodies can't help it.

What physical condition is your character in when he speaks?

French Scenes

Every time a character enters or exits a scene, a new scene has begun.

I don't mean you need to add an extra empty line of white space every time someone enters or exits—I mean that every time someone enters or exits, relationships change, and so does dialogue. In theatre, we call this a *French scene*.

Let's put two teenage girls in one of the girls' bedrooms on a Sunday afternoon. They are gossiping about Hunk Musclechin, all-star quarterback at their school.

Without giving you any more information, can you hear how this conversation sounds?

Let's call this "scene one." Now, Dad enters and asks, "Did you finish your homework?"

Scene two has just begun, because a new character has come into the scene. When Dad leaves, scene two will be over and scene three will begin, because a character—it doesn't matter that it's Dad—has left the scene. (If the daughter or friend left the scene, it would still change to scene three.)

You don't need to number all these entrances and exits in your manuscript (though doing so might yield some interesting patterns you can exploit later). The purpose of identifying a French scene is to take note of how the relationships instantly change when someone enters or exits.

You heard the two girls talking; do you also hear the shift in their voices once Dad enters? Whether in big ways or small, word choice changes; tone changes; expressions change.

And can you hear how those things shift *back* once Dad is gone?

Again: Every time a character enters or exits, the relationships between the remaining characters changes. So should the dialogue.

Create Relationships in Scenes

In *Audition*, Michael Shurtleff makes a wonderful distinction between relationships and a character's status. Writers should be after the former, not the latter.

What's the difference?

If a woman says, "He's my husband," that's a status. It's a title. It tells us nothing about how she feels right *now*.

If she says, "That's my fella!" we've got a different texture; more of a relationship. It's hard to imagine her saying this while frowning deeply. (Although context, of course, plays a large role—maybe there's a reason she'd choose those words to express anger or frustration depending on what's happening in the scene.)

Similarly, a man who introduces his spouse by saying, "This is my wife, Judy," is feeling something much different than if he says, "This is my bride, Judy."

What sort of relationship might it indicate where a man uses the term "bride" rather than "wife?" It means one thing if they were married yesterday; it means quite another if they've been married sixty years.

Go back to our two teens and the dad: don't let the characters simply rely on their status. *She's my daughter. He's my father.* Blah! Right then and there, as the scene unfolds, they are feeling very *specific* things; they are engaged in a very specific relationship. Show it to us in how they interact *right then*.

That relationship, that exact moment in the scene, is powerfully impacted by what we call the Moment Before.

Where is Dad coming from before he enters his daughter's room? Did he just get home after losing his job? Did he just get a raise? Did his team just win, or lose, the Super Bowl?

Where a character was and what he was just doing impacts how he's going to say his first line of dialogue in a scene.

Wins and Losses

We've already discussed how every line of dialogue is about advancing an agenda. Let's build on that idea:

Almost every line of dialogue is a win or a loss for the character who speaks it.

(A win or a loss? Hmm . . . sounds like there must be *conflict!*)

Every line spoken by any character is either a Win—the character gets what she wants; or it is a Loss—the character does not get what she wants.

Dialogue of any kind is a verbal sword fight, with parries, thrusts, advances, and retreats, all calibrated toward winning (obtaining the goal).

Shakespeare, for all his long-windedness, was a master at this. Take a look at Macbeth, Act I, Scene 7. Here, Macbeth tries to get out of murdering King Duncan to take his throne, while Lady Macbeth keeps goading him into it. (I've truncated the scene to remove Shakespeare's wordiness and more easily illustrate the point.)

MACBETH
We will proceed no further in this business:
He [Duncan] hath honour'd me of late.

LADY MACBETH
Art thou afeard
To be the same in thine own act and valour
As thou art in desire?

MACBETH
I dare do all that may become a man.

LADY MACBETH
I have given suck, and know
How tender 'tis to love the babe that milks me:
I would, while it was smiling in my face,
Have pluck'd my nipple from his boneless gums,
And dash'd the brains out, had I so sworn as you
Have done to this.

52

MACBETH
If we should fail?

LADY MACBETH
We fail!
But screw your courage to the sticking-place,
And we'll not fail.

MACBETH
I am settled, and bend up
Each corporal agent to this terrible feat.

Macbeth starts off declaring in no uncertain terms that he will not assassinate the king. Each line he speaks is geared toward that agenda. Likewise, Lady Macbeth craves the throne of Scotland for her husband, so every line she speaks is geared toward *that* agenda. Looking over the scene, you could quite literally write an "L" beside Macbeth's lines and a "W" beside Lady Macbeth's lines to indicate who is winning and losing during the course of the dialogue.

Macbeth changes tactics each time, trying to find an argument that will work against her; she parries expertly back, answering each of his arguments with one of her own. For instance, he tries to say it's more manly to not kill the king; she replies by saying she'd kill their own child if she'd promised him she'd do it. (Yeesh!) It is the collision of their two different Wants that builds tension and raises the stakes.

These are characters who are *fighting for* what they want. If the dialogue looked like this:

LADY MACBETH
Go kill the king.

MACBETH
No.

LADY MACBETH
Yes.

MACBETH
Well, okay.

We're not exactly going to be riveted. There is no struggle, no shift in tactics, to straining to attain the Goal.

In other words: Boring.

Most of the time, your protagonist *should be losing*. That's the point of being a protagonist—getting his or her Wants, Needs, or Goals thwarted at every turn until the very end. Most protagonists win very few encounters until the final climax. Even then, they needn't win; it is the struggle for the goal that keeps readers turning the pages. Antagonists are simply characters who tend to win.

The scene goes on until Macbeth agrees to go through with the murder. Game, set, and match for Lady Macbeth!

Our protagonist suffers a defeat in this scene, because he is unable to conquer the obstacle in front of him. *And the plot moves forward*. Protagonists losing is exactly how plots keep rolling along.

This will be particularly true in contemporary novels lacking direct, explosive action like sword fights, car chases, or gun battles. Like stage plays, these contemporary novels absolutely depend on conflict being expressed with dialogue.

In a speculative genre, some conflicts can (and should) be solved with violence. In a contemporary, non-speculative novel, it must by necessity be sorted out in dialogue.

Blocking

"Blocking" refers to the physical movement of a character.

When someone sits, stands, enters, exits, walks, jumps, shakes his head, rolls her eyes, swings a sword, pulls a trigger, and so on . . . that is their blocking. Blocking is physical action, motivated by emotional responses.

What's that got to do with dialogue? Simple: words are not the only way we communicate. Body language, expressions, and other actions tell us as much—sometimes more—as what is being said or presented. Consider a handshake: We may get one impression of a person based on what he's wearing or what he says, and quite another when we shake his hand.

Blocking is found in the narrative parts of fiction. It can substitute for spoken words, or it can enhance a spoken line. Deciding which to use is the skill we want to develop.

One trick to effectively using blocking with dialogue is to simply avoid doubling up on them, like this:

"I don't know," he shrugged.

Yeah . . . we know what a shrug means. It means "I don't know." There's no reason to write both; no reason to "double up."

Take a look at this exchange:

> **"I told Richard what you said about him," Jenny said.**
> **Susan shot up from the couch, her mouth falling open. "You did *what?*" she screeched.**
> **"You heard me," Jenny said, smiling wickedly.**

(Oh, hey! Note that Jenny is advancing an agenda!)

There's nothing wrong with this exchange of lines and the blocking, although an argument could be made that the adverb is little weak. But doesn't Susan's leap up from the couch—her blocking—clearly indicate what she's thinking? The dialogue works just as well if you eliminate Susan's spoken line and rely only on blocking:

> **"I told Richard what you said about him," Jenny said.**
> **Susan shot up from the couch, her mouth falling open.**
> **"You heard me," Jenny said, smiling wickedly.**

On the other hand, you can also consider *removing* some blocking to keep the dialogue moving at a quicker pace:

> **"I told Richard what you said about him," Jenny said.**

"You did *what?*"

"You heard me," Jenny said, smiling wickedly.

As always, neither choice is right or wrong; it's just something you should take into account during revision.

Give action to your dialogue from time to time to *show* rather than *tell* how the line should be understood. It's the difference between:

Mom ground the heels of her palms into her eyes. "I really can't take this anymore."

And:

"I really can't take this anymore," Mom sobbed.

Both are perfectly acceptable, and I'm not suggesting the first one is necessarily great writing. But that first example is action, and it *shows* us how Mom feels. Using *Mom sobbed* merely *tells* us.

Next: Does the character's blocking reveal anything about the character, plot, or theme? Or is it just moving people around the room? (The two hardest things to do on stage are to move and to stand still!)

Let's change Romeo's blocking in the famous balcony scene, for example:

Instead of having Romeo creep around like a . . . well, *creeper*, imagine he is invited up to the balcony by Juliet right away, and he tells her softly, to her face, perhaps holding her hands, or even whispering in her ear:

But soft . . . what light through yon window breaks? It is the east—and Juliet is the *sun*. Arise, fair sun! And kill the envious moon, who is already sick and pale with grief that thou, her maid, art far more fair than she!

Oo-ah! Feels a lot different, doesn't it? (I have again taken liberties with the punctuation, but that's okay, so do all of Shakespeare's editors. And of course the reference to the *yon window* is a little out of context here, but if it were dialogue in a novel, that is easily remedied; or perhaps the window he refers to is her eyes . . . ?)

The point is this: All we've done is deliberately change Romeo's physical location (blocking) and the text takes on a whole new sensation.

(Sidebar: I actually did make this change for a production of *R&J*, and I gotta tell ya, it was an awesome thing to watch.)

Let's revisit Teen Me and the escape from the police helicopter searchlight. Notice that the punctuation and setting show that extra tags or descriptors or not necessary. We could say:

"Behind the garbage can!" he panted, clutching his chest. "Behind it! Behind it, lift the lid up!"

There's nothing wrong with the blocking. However, unless he is going to literally suffer a heart attack after this, there's no reason for us to see him clutching his chest.

Taking One's Leave

Take a look at Macbeth I:7 again for a moment, and let's build on that Wins and Losses discussion as it pertains to blocking.

What do you notice about their blocking in that scene? Oh, I know, there's no narrative to show us what the characters are doing, but picture them in your mind. Macbeth and Lady Macbeth having this argument . . . going round and round . . . he says he doesn't want to hurt the king, she says he must.

What's odd about this conversation? Think about it for a second.

Got it figured out?

Macbeth doesn't leave.

Here's a decorated combat veteran who's been publicly praised by the king of his nation. No pushover, this guy. When Lady Macbeth suggests killing the king so Macbeth can assume the throne, if Macbeth truly didn't like that idea, guess what? He's one "Silence, woman!" away from ending the plot right then and there.

But he doesn't. He stays in the room and has the argument. What does his blocking (his *lack* of leaving the room) reveal?

That maybe . . . he kinda, sorta, possibly . . . *wants* to be convinced to assassinate his king?

I bring this up because it's a common motivation problem actors have during scene work. It can also afflict authors who ask their characters, "What do you want in this scene?"

Since conflict is at the heart of every plot, and dialogue the mechanism by which the plot moves forward, much theatre dialogue is based on verbal arguments or disagreements. When the director asks, "What do you want in this scene?" and the actor replies, "I just want to leave the room," he's chosen the weakest possible motivation.

Why? Because nine times out of ten, no one is physically forcing him to stay. If his Want is to leave the room, in most cases, he can simply leave the dang room.

Now in a thriller novel, let's say, where the protagonist has been captured by the bad guys and is chained up against a wall, it's perfectly reasonable for his Want to be, "I want to leave the room!"

In a contemporary story, however, it's simply not enough for the character to want to "leave the room." Otherwise he would.

Think about real-life domestic squabbles. How often do we get to the point where we actually walk away? And how often is the attempt to walk away physically thwarted? (Of course, sadly, this does happen in some homes—but I trust that most of us have only to deal with some general bickering or arguments.)

We often stay in the fight. Because why? *We want something from our opponent.* (See how it all comes back to those goals?)

Unless someone puts a gun to our head, we're usually perfectly capable of leaving an argument—we just don't, because we want to Win.

And, as one more loose thread to tie up, can you see where a domestic argument emphasizes the difference between status and relationship? Frank may love his wife Judy, but if they're fighting about why they don't go out anymore, their relationship in the scene isn't "husband and wife." Their status hasn't changed, their relationship has.

Shurtleff says actors should make choices that allow for "maximum possible involvement." Don't allow your characters to get away with using "I want to leave the room" as a motivation; leaving is the opposite of involvement. It's disengagement, and it's not interesting.

Relationships, blocking, setting . . . all these things dress the stage—your story—for outstanding dialogue.

Part Two Q & A

Q: How do I know I'm using the right setting for a scene?

A: If the scene seems to be working for you, an editor, an agent, and readers, it's the right setting.

Okay, that was cheeky, I apologize. There's no easy answer because every single scene ever written is different, and every single scene ever written could theoretically be set somewhere else.

Ask yourself these questions:

Is the setting having an emotional or at least dramatic impact?

Is this a logical place for the scene to take place under the given circumstances of the novel?

Does the place I've chosen have any thematic resonance?

If all else fails, rewrite the scene in a different location and see what happens. (This is not a bad exercise, regardless of whether you keep the results or not.)

I do urge caution in defying standard genre expectations; mysteries, thrillers, romances, fantasy, science fiction, and everything in between tend to have readers with certain criteria in their minds, whether they know it or not. For example, if your romance takes place on a sprawling ranch in the 1800s, the big climax (*ahem!*) between the two leads is maybe best suited to an open prairie under a lovely Texas sky, rather than in a stuffy old schoolhouse—unless the stuffy old schoolhouse has some sort of thematic meaning.

Exercises

1. Print out several pages of your manuscript (or the whole thing), and mark each Win and Loss with a pencil. It's not a huge deal if you can't do it for each and every single line of dialogue, but if you've got a page or more where you can't find any, it's time to rethink the scene.

2. Take a scene that you're unsure of or that needs work. Rewrite it set in one of these places, and/or come up with some of your own. Don't worry about the internal logic of the story for this ("There are no golf courses in my dystopian YA!"). An odd setting is part of the point. Just freewrite and see what you discover.

A) A golf course at night during a thunderstorm.
B) An outpost on Europa, looking out at Jupiter.
C) A prison cell.
D) The food court of a mall.
E) On a rooftop watching fireworks in the distance.
F) Front row of a house of worship, during a service.
G) Trapped: ski lift, elevator, broom closet, whatever.

PART THREE – ON THE PAGE

Should You Say Said?

All right, let's get busy.

You've built a great plot with great conflict into great scenes. Let's start getting into the nitty-gritty stuff, like whether to use "said" or "screamed," whether and when and how to use dialect, how to use contractions, punctuation, and different fonts . . . here we go!

Tags: He Said, She Said

First, an answer to the question that made you buy this book:

"How often should I use *he said* or *she said*?"

The answer is:

There is no rule.

Sorry.

What *I, personally* recommend is using "said" (as opposed to another tag like murmured, shrieked, etc.) about 75% of the time. Sometimes, a character simply must cough, breathe, sigh, shout, scream, mutter, mumble, or groan a line.

It's okay! I hereby give you permission to use those tags as needed.

But select those deviations from *said* deliberately. Realize that every time you use an alternative to "said," the reader pauses just a bit. It's almost imperceptible, but it happens; it takes the brain just that teeny bit longer to adjust to a word other than "said," which we gloss right over.

In fact, one reason to default to "said" is because we *want* it to be glossed over, so the reader can charge right on through the rest of the scene. Anything other than "said" gives the reader a slight pause. If that's what you are after, great. If it's not, be careful.

Some authors encourage the percentage of "said" usage to be closer to 90 or even 99% of the time. But it should rarely if ever dip below 75% for a novel, no matter the genre.

One other argument about this sticky topic goes something like this:

"Don't use 'said' at all. End the line of dialogue, then use a bit of physical action or blocking." Roughly speaking, it's the difference between:

"We have to do something about this," Bill said, frowning.

and

Bill frowned. "We have to do something about this."

or

"We have to do something about this," Bill frowned.

These are all fine, and I understand the suggestion to rephrase dialogue without that old *said* tag hanging around. So use your own judgement, but don't do both:

Bill frowned. "We have to do something about this," he said.

That's simply too wordy and cluttered. Any of the other three examples is a little more elegant.

A word of caution on getting rid of every use of "said" is in order here. I once encountered an unpublished manuscript where the word "said" simply and utterly did not exist— *anywhere*— and it really threw me for a loop. I never did get accustomed to it not being there. In that particular case, the word's *absence* was more distracting than its inclusion would have been. So in all things, moderation.

Be Logical

Double and triple check your tags to ensure they are logical. For example:

"Get down!" he hissed.

He hissed makes no real-world sense here, simply because *GeT DowN* can't be hissed; those consonants are just too hard-edged to *hissssss*. The onomatopoeia doesn't match.

Now, you might get away with:

"Sit!" he hissed.

because the sibilance is in the same ballpark despite the hard "T" consonant.

Similarly:

"Your attitude has been extremely poor these past few weeks, and I have had it up to here with you!" Mom barked.

is a little hard to accept; Mom must be really on the scent of something important to "bark" so many syllables! "Bark" has a quick, sharp quality to it—like "hiss," it has great onomatopoeia.

So something more like this:

"Go!" Mom barked.

sounds like a bark. One syllable, one hard consonant. But try to combine the two examples and you end up with:

"Go!" Mom hissed.

Ew. Can you feel how awkward that is? How it sort of jars the eye and ear?

Aim for logical tags when you're doing your revision.

Ways People Speak

Word choice and the cadence, or rhythm, of speech varies widely from person to person. It's actually fairly simple to differentiate characters by making intentional choices about these qualities.

How a character speaks shows the reader a lot about that character, and care should be taken to ensure you're not misleading the reader (unless of course, you're misleading them on purpose). Geographical background, upbringing, education, emotional state . . . these all impact how we speak.

Word Choice

Perhaps the most obvious way to differentiate characters is in their word choice. Is the character prone to multisyllabic words like *multisyllabic*?

Or does he just kinda talk real regular?

Neither is wrong, but both reveal character. Readers will be inclined to associate big words with intelligence or education, and shorter words with—well, less than that. However, your evil mastermind might be exceedingly sharp but conceal it with small words, while your total idiot might try to mask his imbecilic nature with big but improperly used words. (Dogberry in *Much Ado About Nothing* is a classic example.)

Ask yourself: Would this character say the skyscraper was *big*, or *colossal*? The words are practically synonymous, but what they say about the character is different.

Listen closely to how different people speak in real life. Really parse people's speech. Many young people don't use the word "angry," for instance. Most of them (and many of us) still fall back on the word "mad," or even "pissed." Neither is terribly good English, but then American speech isn't proper.

On the other hand, a half-orc cleric in a fantasy novel probably should not use "pissed" when he's really angry. (There are always exceptions, of course!)

(Furthermore, be aware that many words have different meanings in the United States than they do in other nations—"pissed" being one of them.)

Tics & Favorites

I define "tics" as those strange little quirks of language and speech individuals have that can be used in fiction to help identify a character.

One example from *Party* is a character named Daniel, who has a tendency to call everyone "soldier," for no particular reason specified in the novel. It's just a Daniel Thing.

We all have favorite words and phrases we've picked up; so too might your characters. It could be a catchphrase, like "We're gonna have to roll sixes!" or else a word that seems to keep cropping up. (I happen to like "colossal" and use it far more than is truly necessary.) (Have you noticed?)

Again, these choices should be deliberate. (You've seen that word like 10 times now, I hope a pattern is emerging!) One of my favorite "secrets" about my novel *Zero* is about exactly this sort of intentionality.

Zero follows the exploits of a young visual artist, Amanda, and her boyfriend Mike, who is a musician. You know how when we are trying to get someone's attention or make a specific point, we say words like, "Look!" or "Listen!" before the declaration? As in, "Listen, I did my homework like you asked!"

In *Zero*, Amanda will only use the word "Look," and Mike will only use the word "Listen." Get it?

Artist . . . musician . . .
Look . . . listen . . . ?

It's a small thing. No one notices it unless I point it out. But it's there, and *your brain knows it.* If in the last chapter, Mike suddenly said, "Look, I need this job" instead of "Listen, I need this job," trust me, there'd be a teeny little glitch in your reading when you saw it. I've spent the whole novel training your brain to know that if someone says "Look," but I don't give you an attribution like "Amanda said," you'll still know it's her. Cool, right? *Right?!*

Ahem. Anyway. Whether it's cool or not isn't the point—the point is, it's an intentional choice, the type you should make as you revise your dialogue.

I don't encourage characters using their tics and favorites on every page, or even necessarily more than once every couple of chapters. Use these tic like salt—as a nice seasoning, but not so much that it'll ruin the flavor of everything around it.

When examining your characters' tics, consider: What words might he emphasize? De-emphasize? Does she trail off? What's appropriate to her age? Does he end declarative statements with questions, like, "It was a great movie, wasn't it?"

Sentence Length

Sentence length is another way to differentiate characters. In my novel *Mercy Rule*, which has multiple first-person narrators in each chapter, it became critical that I make each voice distinct.

Let's take one single sentence, and show how different characters might say them in the novel. The sentence is:

I woke up, got ready for the day, and walked to school.

Here's how some of the characters in *Mercy Rule* might say it:

BRADY
Got up. Got ready. Walked to school.

CADENCE
I woke up and got ready for the day and walked to school.

DANNY
I woke the hell up, got ready for the goddam day, and walked to goddam school.

Very different sentences. Each conveys the same information, though. What kind of assumptions do you make about someone speaking the way these characters do? While I can't control how you perceive the characters, I'd be willing to bet whatever your assumptions are, you're either right on or very close to the way I *want* you to perceive them.

Obviously, I've thrown grammar out the window at this point—or I've defenestrated it, if you wish. So realize, too, that a character who *does* speak with proper grammar has a different voice of her own, provided not everyone in your story also speaks that way.

Having Contractions

One thing I see a lot in first-time writers is a lack of contractions. This mystifies me. Americans contract *everything*! Contractions can be grammatically correct, such as:

isn't for is not
couldn't for could not

Or somewhat less correctly but widely accepted:

gonna for going to
kinda for kind of
coulda for could have*

Then there's dropping off the ends of words, usually a G:

drinkin' for drinking
smokin' for smoking

I recommend this last example for use in dialogue exclusively (rather than in narrative), unless your novel is first person and you don't think the narrative will get bogged down with so many contractions. Like dialect, this sort of thing can be fun, but in small doses.

*Friendly reminder! Be careful when contracting two words ending in "of."

kind of = kinda
could have = coulda
sort of = sorta
could of = WRONG

"Could of" is neither a contraction nor grammatically correct, *ever*, in the printed word. This is an ear-to-page translation error. We hear the "v" sound, and mistake it for "of" instead of "have."

So you have multiple choices with contractions. Be deliberate with those choices. Should your character say *could have*, or *could've*, or *coulda?* Each has a different syntax. And again, it depends on things like scenario; the relationship the speaker has with the others who are present; physical and mental state; and so on.

In addition to first-time writers avoiding contractions, I am especially perplexed when some fiction writers make a standard-issue American teenager say:

I could have gone to the party, but I did not.

Srsly? Most of us, teen or not, would say aloud:

"I coulda gone to the party, but I didn't."

By and large, American diction is pretty sloppy if we're not giving a speech of some kind, or formally trained in elocution (actors, politicians, etc.). Most of us would probably say:

"I could've gone to the party, but I didn't."

If, on the other hand, I spelled out those phrases that would typically be contractions, there better be a reason, like the character is trying to make a point:

"Mom," I said patiently, "I could have gone to the party, but I did not."

See how the narrator chooses *not* to use contractions, so that maybe Mom will actually hear his point? In fact, I'd even consider deleting the modifier "patiently" here, because the character's deliberate choice to not use contractions speaks to his goal, tone, and state of mind without it.

"Mom, I could have gone to the party, but I did not."

Can you hear his tone just as well without using the modifier?

Accents, Foreign and Domestic

Writing accents is a tricky endeavor. The temptation is to spell accented words phonetically. I've done it myself. I also sometimes wish I hadn't in some cases.

There's no real right or wrong answer to the question of spelling accents phonetically, but I do urge extreme caution.

Using them poorly can be offensive, or worse. On the other hand, like all of these suggestions, the right amount at the right time can have a big impact.

One good example: In *Bastard Out of Carolina*, author Dorothy Allison uses "an't" for "ain't," or isn't. That's just about the only accented English to be found in the entire novel, but it gives just the right flavor of its time and place without being overwrought. She strikes an excellent balance between phonetics, accent, and authentic voice.

Another issue on accents is simply this: Who's to say someone *has* an accent? And can you tell regional differences? To me, born and raised in Arizona, "Southern accents" all sound alike. That could be as near as Texas and as far as the Virginias. I am certain that folks from both areas would be quick to correct my southwestern stupidity. And never mind what my ridiculous Phoenician accent must sound like to *them*. Would someone from geographic area "X" agree that how you wrote the accent is in fact the way it sounds?

Maybe it's enough to say *She had a delightful southern lilt* or *His voice had a rough, Irish sean-nós quality*, and let it go at that, using regional words and phrases to fill in and do the job phonetics would otherwise do. It's often wiser to rely on regional word choice and/or word placement to show a regional accent.

Additionally, if you're not personally familiar with a geographic accent, you're probably basing the impulse to write phonetically on things you've heard in movies and on television. That's risky, too, because who's to say the actors or director got it right?

Discretion is the better part of writing accents. If you do choose to use some kind of phonetics to illustrate accent, try doing so sparingly; there's no need to beat readers over the head, as in Irvine Welsh's *Trainspotting*, though it is a great book and a great primer on how to write phonetic Scots—but again, those accents are particular to certain geographical locations within Scotland. To an American, there may only be a "Scottish accent" or an "English accent." To Scots and Britons, there are numerous accents, just as Americans don't have one standardized "American accent."

Sometimes, it's enough to draw attention to an accent or vocal tic, then let it go. I have a dear friend who has the world's most pronounced glottal stop. She would say *We're meeting by the fountain on the mountain* like this: "We're mee'in' by the foun'in on the mou'in." You don't want to have to read that quirk throughout an entire novel; pointing it out when we first meet such a character and then writing the words correctly (rather than phonetically) thereafter is usually fine.

(On the other hand, very few of us pronounce the T sound in words like *button*, so . . . potayto, potahto.)

Such a pronounced tic ought to impact the character or even plot in some way. For better or worse, it should be a *useful* tic (for you, the author) in terms of the storytelling.

You're Not From Around Here, Are You?

To the best of your ability, be aware of regional word choice. The most famous example, perhaps, is "pop" versus "soda." An awareness of regional words is particularly tricky if you are writing about a region you haven't so much as visited.

Bear in mind that while transplants from one part of the country (or world) (or *worlds?*) sometimes adopt the regional words of their new homes after a year or so, they might retain long-held words or phrases that will set them apart in your story. That's something else you can use to distinguish voice—the guy who always says "pop" instead of "soda" or whatever.

Apart from moving to a new state for a year or two to study the local linguistics, the following Harvard Dialect Study website can be a real asset. It's a large but not comprehensive list of regional words and phrases. Don't stick to it slavishly—use it as a reference.

www4.uwm.edu/FLL/linguistics/dialect/maps.html

Punctuation

Punctuation is your best friend (or worst enemy) when it comes to dialogue. Punctuation is like reading notes in music, with each mark having a specific function and "sound" on the page.

Not everyone will agree with me on this, which is fine. But this is my opinion and I'm sticking to it:

Punctuation is how you guide your reader in how to "hear" a line of prose, whether in dialogue or narrative.

(We'll talk more about narration in a bit.)

Like musical notes conduct a musician on what note should be played, punctuation guides our readers to "hearing" the voice you want them to hear on the page.

Consider: The period versus the question mark! The rules say we put a question mark at the end of a question. Cool; I don't disagree with that. And nine times out of ten, if your character asks a question, you ought probably use a question mark to show it. If we're talking about writing essays for Harvard? It's probably a good way to go.

Consider the period versus the question mark. The rules say we put a question mark at the end of a question. Cool. I don't disagree with that! And, nine times out of ten, if your character asks a question you ought probably use a question mark to show it. If we're talking about writing essays for Harvard . . . it's probably a good way to go.

Astute readers have just noticed that the previous two paragraphs were nearly identical. I apologize for being sneaky, but can you now go back and notice how you read each one just a bit differently based on the changes in punctuation? Some of the punctuation used is wrong by grammatical rules, but I do not care. What I care about is clarity and voice. Did one paragraph *make more sense* than the other? I hope not. Did they both "sound" the same to you as you read? Probably not.

Bottom line, we are not writing essays, here. We're writing fiction or scripts, and we're talking about crafting authentic characters within that fiction, and sometimes? People uptick the end of statements. Like I just did there.

And you knew how to read it.

You, the reader, knew how *I*, the author, wanted that sentence to be read. That's the power of punctuation.

Types of Punctuation

These are the "notes" we have available in our music of dialogue and prose. Please note I am including different types of font in our punctuation discussion.

period	.
comma	,
em-dash	——
semicolon	;
colon	:
ellipsis	…
exclamation	!
question	?
parentheses	( ) [and brackets, etc.]
strike ~~outs~~	font
bold	font
italics	font
CAPS	font

What Punctuation Is Used For

When it comes to dialogue and narration, what purpose does punctuation serve? Put simply:

To indicate a length and type of pause.

One of the first things I was taught to do in my Shakespeare training was to remove all the punctuation from the script. For one thing, any modern rendering is being punctuated by someone from the modern age, and so can sometimes be arbitrary. Also, the punctuation used by editors—or even the punctuation Shakespeare used in his day—may not indicate how you actually want to perform the line to a 21st Century audience. (See the *Henry V* example in "Setting.")

For example, in the New Folger Library Shakespeare edition of *Macbeth*, (Washington Square Press, 1992) we find this line, spoken by Macbeth right after having killed the king:

What hands are here! Ha, they pluck out mine eyes.

Whereas the MIT.edu full text collection of Shakespeare's plays renders the same line thusly:

What hands are here? ha! they pluck out mine eyes.

And the *Applause First Folio of Shakespeare Comedies, Histories & Tragedies in Modern Type* (Folio Scripts, 2001) renders it like this:

What Hands are here? hah: they pluck out mine Eyes.

None of these is right or wrong, but as the actor (or director), how would you want the word heard and understood?

Consider these variations on the same line:

What hands are here . . . ? ha. they pluck out mine eyes.

What hands are here! ha—they pluck out mine eyes.

What hands are here? *ha*! they pluck out mine eyes!

What hands are here? Ha! *They pluck out mine eyes.*

Or, my personal favorite, perhaps delivered by William Shatner:

What . . . *hands* are here? ha! they . . . pluck *out* mine . . . *eyes*!

Bottom line: A semicolon isn't the same type of pause as an em dash, or as an ellipsis, and so on.

Here's a real-life example from my zombie novel *Sick*. This is how the line appears in the book, as my protagonist tries to convince a friend that his buddy Jack shouldn't be left behind to die:

That was Jack, Jack was out there, we gotta let him in.

The copyeditor wanted it written with periods instead:

That was Jack. Jack was out there. We gotta let him in.

Now, you can have your opinion of course, but I read the first example in rush, because there are no periods. On the page, it flows together and sounds desperate. (To me, anyway. Also notice, the copyeditor did not change "gotta" to "we have to." *Gotta* sounds like a hurry, doesn't it?)

Here's another real-life example of where I differed with a copyeditor on punctuation, this from my novel *Random*. Read these two silently, then aloud. See if you hear a difference between:

Otherwise, you wouldn't have made a call like this.

And:

Otherwise you wouldn't have made a call like this.

I believe the first one is grammatically correct, and that's how the copyeditor wanted it changed. Had it been in narrative, I probably would've made the change and moved on. But when I see that comma there, that changes the musicality of the line; how it sounds in the ear, whether spoken aloud or read silently. Taking into account the scene's setting, mood, characters—all that good stuff—I felt that keeping the comma slowed things down. Not much, but enough.

I am not advocating filling your manuscript with an assortment of punctuation just for the sake of it (though you might not know it to look at my published work). Periods and commas are always going to be your primary weapons, just like using "he said, she said" are most often your best dialogue tags.

Using "Said" With Punctuation

We talked about how punctuation acts as musical notes of a sort. Word choice and the order of those words also impacts flow; it changes how a reader reads narrative and dialogue.

Let's revisit our previous discussion about how often to use "said" (or "says") when you look at these next two examples from *Hellworld*, in which one of the heroes is arguing with an old professor that there must be some chance of saving the world from an impending apocalypse:

"There's got to be a way!" Charlie shouts.

Dr. Riley calmly swigs from his tequila bottle, and smacks his lips afterward with a sigh.

"If I thought that," he says, "I wouldn't be out here with a gun I've never fired once in my entire life."

Another way to render this set of dialogue is like this:

"There's got to be a way!" Charlie shouts.

Dr. Riley calmly swigs from his tequila bottle, and smacks his lips afterward with a sigh. "If I thought that, I wouldn't be out here with a gun I've never fired once in my entire life."

As I'm sure you've realized by now, either one is fine. Notice, though, how in the first version, there's a *forced pause* on Dr. Riley's line. By including "he says" in the line, I'm physically forcing the reader to hesitate. (Kind of neat, huh? The power we have?)

That hesitation, no matter how tiny, gives the line just that *little bit* more suspense; a *little bit* more of a wait before Riley admits the situation is hopeless. At this point in the story, we want Riley to give the heroes a course of action, a solution. The suspense builds . . . then *nothing*. Riley will be no help at all, and maybe things really are as grim as we fear. (Keep those stakes going up, remember!)

Read the samples again. Can you hear it? The second example runs together; things keep right on going. That's great for a faster-paced scene, but this one needed some cooling off, some slow burn. So I opted for the first iteration.

Here's another example from *Hellworld* of punctuation changing inflection, and therefore, mood and tone.

"I don't see where we stand much chance," Dr. Riley says.
"So that's it," Charlie says. "That's all you got."

Grammatically, Charlie's lines seem like they should end with question marks. But question marks go "up" at the end. Periods go "down." *Down* is how I want the delivery to sound in the reader's head. Imagine these words on a sheet of music. It's the difference between:

                                             got?
           it?   you
    that's   all
So   That's

And:

So   That's
   that's   all
     it.   you
                     got.

Both of these marks indicate how a line of dialogue might sound. A period is declarative; the sentence is over. An exclamation is also declarative, but has a bite at the end! In this example, I felt the periods conveyed not only a sense of finality, but of hopelessness on Charlie's part, where question marks could have sounded a bit, dare I say, whiny.

These are intentional choices designed to guide your eye and ear to how the line might be said, or read. Consider using these nontraditional marks from time to time to give each character a unique voice. Just don't use them arbitrarily.

The Font of Knowledge

Let's close up this section with a quick word on typefaces and fonts:

Use caution.

Okay, that was two words, but I stand by them.

When formatting a fiction manuscript for submission to an agent or editor, it's best to use the then-current standard font for emphasis. As of this writing—and unlikely to change soon—that standard is *italics*.

There are plenty of examples of novels (including my own) where underlines and bold fonts, in addition to italics, are used in an attempt to produce one sort of emphasis or another. (Both *Party* and *Zero* are good examples of how I used them.) In my short story *Survival Instinct* in the collection *Violent Ends*, for example, I rendered an abusive father character's dialogue in bold font exclusively, without any quotation marks. These were corrected by a copyeditor to be standard font and with quotation marks; then *re-*corrected back to the original way by both myself and the collection's editor, Shaun Hutchinson. Both of us felt the bolding was the right choice for the "voice" of the piece.

But generally, stick with italics for emphasis rather than bold. (Do as I say, not as I do!) (Unless of course what you do is working, in which case, carry on.)

Using other typefaces entirely—such as Arial or Comic Sans and so on—rather than a conventional typeface carries a risk generally not worth taking. Times New Roman is the accepted typeface to use for manuscripts, with Courier New being a distant second. (My understanding is Courier 12-point is still the default for screenplays; stage plays have no such standard, but don't deviate from Courier or Times.)

Seriously, if you're submitting to New York houses or agents you want to represent you, do not mess around with typefaces for an entire manuscript. (I mean, you *can*, but do so to your own peril. You've been warned.)

If, on the other hand, you're going the indie route, then please do your due diligence on what makes a good typeface for e-readers and for print. I am not *about* to get into that discussion here. Do your homework.

(For what it's worth, for readers of the print version of this book, I'm using Garamond 12.5-point font. But for formatting independent books, there are other issues to consider, like spacing, letting . . . yeah. Do your research, Indies.)

Part Three Q & A

Q: Since most Americans use contractions, should all of my characters always use spellings like coulda, woulda, *and* shoulda?

A: No. These are tools in your dialogue toolbox. You need to pick the right tool to get the job done. I might be willing to argue that most American characters should use the contractions *could've*, *would've*, and *should've*, yes. These are grammatically correct, and have "less voice" than those ending with "a." Having one character use *coulda* and other contracted words ending in "a" is probably enough.

Q: You got awfully specific about things like commas. Isn't that a little overboard?

A: When you get your first round of line edits from a professional copyeditor, you'll be amazed at how specific you suddenly must become. So the answer is No, it's not a little overboard—at least not for a New York publisher. They will question every single little detail, details you might not have even been aware were in your manuscript. Gird up, it's gonna be a long day of copyediting (no matter what).

If you're going indie, maybe it *might* not matter so much, but I still maintain that punctuation should be a deliberate choice made during manuscript revision to best obtain the voice you want to capture and share in the pages.

Q: You talked about using logic with tags. What about tags that are physically impossible, such as: "It's so dusty!" Bob sneezed. Can or should I use those?

A: Some authors or editors would argue here that a person cannot literally sneeze and talk at the same time, ergo, writers should not use a dialogue tag such as *sneezed*. I see the point here, and would probably veer away from such usages, but it would not trip me up, personally. It's your call.

What you must do, though, is *be aware* that you've used an "impossible" tag, and accept any consequences.

Q: You said not to use unconventional typefaces for an entire *manuscript; can I used them sparingly, like for chapter headings, or other characters's voices, or to show a handwritten journal entry, or to distinguish between narrators in a multiple-POV novel?*

A: Good catch, and great question.

First, do not use "fun" typefaces for chapter headings. It just looks amateurish. Let professional designers do that job.

Second, I understand the temptation to use different typefaces for different characters in a multi-POV. I do not recommend it. For starters, your writing alone should be enough to differentiate one character from another. Also, as above, typeface is a book designer's job, not an author's. Your job is to deliver clarity above all else, not gimmicks.

For short (one page or less) journal entries or other "handwriting" that you want to show in your prose, or for text messages and so on that will be portrayed in print, stick with italics. That's the standard. Sell your novel first, then talk design specifics with your editor when the time comes.

Exercises

1. Choose a scene from your manuscript, and take one character from it who you're not writing his or her dialogue phonetically, and re-write it with phonetics. Forced to see and read how Frank or Judy actually sound out loud, what did you discover about them? (Maybe nothing—that's an acceptable answer.) Or does it turn out that in your head, you've heard Judy wrongly hitting a syllable on a word which drives Frank's Ivy League sensibilities crazy, thus contributing to their divorce?

2. Have a high school, college, or local theatre friend read your manuscript or scenes from your story out loud to you, or have them record it and send it to you. How's it sound? Are things landing just right? Try not to critique the performance itself; listen close for how the actor instinctively followed the "musical notes" (punctuation, etc.) in your prose. Ask her questions afterward to further clarify anything that didn't sound the way you'd wanted it to.

PART FOUR – NARRATION

We've already touched on narration a bit in the preceding sections (such as in Blocking), but it deserves a little more attention for one reason: Whether in first person or third, your novel has a *voice*, and in a sense, that voice is a type of dialogue. You'll want to exercise the same control over narration as you do between Frank and Judy's verbal exchange at the café.

Mileage Out of Narrative Blocking

Remember: blocking is any physical action a character takes.

We've already talked about how and why you should not double up on blocking and dialogue, but can *narrative* blocking enhance dialogue?

Absolutely. Let's take a look:

"Go to your room!" Dad stormed, slamming the door shut.

Nothing wrong with that, it's perfectly legit. The tag "stormed" is a tad overwrought, but appropriate to the blocking of slamming the door shut.

But what about this, instead?

"Go to your room!" Dad kicked the door shut, his work boot leaving a hole the size of my face in the flimsy wood.

Ah-ha. With one line of narrative blocking, we can guess—and probably be right if the author is doing his job—many things about the setting and about Dad.

1. Dad doesn't merely "slam" or "shut" the door, he *kicks* it. Kicking is a decidedly more violent action.

2. Dad is not wearing patent leather wingtips, nor high-end running shoes, nor Birkenstock sandals. He's wearing work boots. There may be many reasons for that, but for now, this detail gives readers a certain impression of what kind of employment he might have (or be looking for).

3. A hole the size of what? Any hole would be bad enough; this is a hole the size of *my face*. This detail further implicates Dad as a man capable of violence.

4. Is the door made of oak? No. It's "flimsy wood." Chances are good we're not in a palatial spread in Beverly Hills.

Given all the clues in just this one piece of narrative blocking, do you already have a picture in mind of not only who Dad is, but where he and the narrator might live?

Having said all that, there's also nothing wrong with being economical and simply writing:

"Go to your room!"

We all know that voice, we've all heard it before. No tags are necessary unless Mom *and* Dad are in the room, and both are actively engaged (speaking) in the scene. If Mom's just sitting quietly on the sofa, or it's just Dad and his kid, we can assume Dad said it, and *how* he said it.

Buying Up Real Estate

How you use your available *white space* has a huge (colossal!) impact on your dialogue and narration. White space is literally that: any place on the printed page where there is no printing. Like punctuation, you must know how to be intentional with your white space. White space is also called *real estate*, and for good reason: Location is everything!

Hard Returns And White Space

Here is the first page of *Party*, as published.

I'm the girl nobody knows until she commits suicide. Then suddenly everyone had a class with her.

You know the one I mean.

You don't pick on her because you don't know she's there, not really. She sits behind you in chemistry, or across the room in Spanish. You've seen her naked in the locker room after physical education—a contradiction in terms if ever there was one—but you don't know what color her eyes are.

What her name is.

What grade she's in.

Remember, a hard return occurs any time a new paragraph has begun. Any time you hit "enter" on your keyboard, you've inserted a hard return.

Now let's play around with our white space a little bit. What if we delete every hard return, and just make it one paragraph? Note that I have not changed a single word or piece of punctuation:

I'm the girl nobody knows until she commits suicide. Then suddenly everyone had a class with her. You know the one I mean. You don't pick on her because you don't know she's there, not really. She sits behind you in chemistry, or across the room in Spanish. You've seen her naked in the locker room after physical education—a contradiction in terms if ever there was one—but you don't know what color her eyes are. What her name is. What grade she's in.

The flow is completely different. Is there an emotional difference? Do you react in a slightly different way than you did at the first iteration?

The first version has a certain cadence to it that the second version does not. In fact, to me, it's almost as if in the second version, the narrator just wants to get this information out of the way. In the first, she seems to be taking her time, making sure the reader gets each individual point she's trying to make.

Point of View

Every novel has a point of view (POV), and the world should be seen through that point of view.

You already know that POV includes the decision to use first-person, third-person limited, or third person omniscient narration, but that's not all I mean by POV here.

Even when writing from the third person omniscient POV, your novel will have that "voice" we talked about earlier;

something in the style that distinguishes your writing from mine, mine from Stephen King, and so on.

And of course, your characters are speaking from a specific point of view of their own, too.

In both cases, it's important to "stay within" the POV you have established.

For example, let's say you are a thirty-something guy writing a contemporary young adult novel written third person from a teenage girl's perspective. (Oh, all right, I'm talking about an earlier draft of *Zero.)*

How the protagonist describes the mountain she can see from her driveway must sound like a teen girl, not a thirty-something guy.

Even shifting to use first person, the rule remains: She has to talk, act, and narrate things in as authentic a way as possible for her character, not in the way the author would do those things.

My first agent once told me, "Only use metaphors and similes your character would use."

Good advice. You should take it, too.

PART FIVE – CONCLUSIONS

Thanks for reading! I hope you've enjoyed the book, and found it at least mildly entertaining and wildly informative.

But before you go, there's one last important thing about writing fiction and crafting dialogue you need to know.

The Black Box

In theatre, the term "black box" has a couple of related meanings. It could refer to a large room painted black, hence becoming a black box, in which performances or rehearsals are held.

Or, a play could be performed as a "black box production," meaning there are few or no special costumes, props, or scenery. Often, this is interpreted literally, with wooden crates painted black serving as all the furniture, and actors wearing only black clothing. Some of the best performances I've ever seen were done black box.

Now, there's nothing wrong with paying good money to see a spectacle on stage—like *The Lion King*, for example, or *Les Miserables*, or *Miss Saigon* with its on-stage helicopter landing. That's what we pay to see.

However:

If the performers can't stand on stage dressed in their street clothes and belt out the songs without accompaniment, be heard, *and* entertain us, then no amount of "spectacle" will help the show.

Your story is the same way.

If you cannot tell a compelling story with only periods and commas and quotation marks; with standard fonts and typefaces; with standard use of white space and proper grammar . . .

Then no amount of "spectacle" will help it.

See what I'm getting at?

All the techniques we've looked at in this book are designed to help you broaden your horizons as a storyteller. They are extra tools that I hope you'll find useful.

But not every tool is right for every job. Take chances, yes; find and use your own voice, absolutely. But do so after having a firm grasp of the black box: stripped down, bare bones, and a great performance.

The Hardest Advice I Ever Give

Well, it's the hardest to hear if not the hardest to say, anyway:

Until your protagonist cashes a royalty check, you are creator-god of this story, and you say who speaks and who doesn't; who lives and who doesn't.

In other words: Your characters have to audition for you, and you have to pick the best ones to make up your cast.

I'm saying this because you shelled out money to read this book. You shelled out *time* you can't ever have back to read this book. I want to give you your money and time's worth, so here it is:

Writing and publishing for money is about craft, and business, and art.

What order you want to put them in is up to you, but it is always about all three. And you must, absolutely must make changes and revisions that benefit the story. Sometimes that means deleting entire characters, or entire chapters. It might mean utterly reworking one character's dialogue and voice. Sometimes it means scrapping draft one and starting over. But whatever it means, remember this:

Story above all.

Whatever you've learned from this book, use it to make your story stronger, no matter what the story must give up in order to make it so.

And of course, as always:

Keep writing!

GLOSSARY

accent - a vocal inflection or tone, and/or the stresses and unstresses used in the spoken language of a regional people group

black box - a stripped-down version of a theatrical performance; used here to mean "do not rely on font or punctuation gimmicks to sell your story"

cadence - rhythmic sequence of sounds in a spoken language

dialect - spoken language of a particular area with its own variations on grammar, word choice, and pronunciation

diction - the way words are used in spoken language

rhythm - repeated patterns of sounds

syntax - the way words are put together into sentences

Did I miss anything? Still have questions, or even corrections? Talk to me at:

facebook.com/AuthorTomLeveen

or on Twitter @tomleveen.

I offer short critiques on the two most important parts of your novel: page one, or the query letter sent to agents. For a personal critique of your first page—the one that will determine if an agent or editor will keep reading—or your query letter, contact me at

www.fiverr.com/tomleveen

About the Author

Tom Leveen is the author of six novels with legacy publishers, all for the young adult market. He is a frequent speaker and teacher at junior high and high schools, colleges and universities, conferences, and the like. He is a native of Arizona, where he lives with his wife and son.

Made in the USA
San Bernardino, CA
17 December 2019